P9-AEV-997

Dear Friend,

We are in the midst of an all-out spiritual war for the next generation! By attending a FamilyLife Conference, participating in an "I Still Do™" event, or listening regularly to our radio program "FamilyLife Today," you have taken a bold stand for your marriage and home. We commend you for this and encourage you to become even more engaged in the battle for the family. As Amy Carmichael wrote, "We have all of eternity to celebrate the victories but only a few hours before sunset." Time is slipping away.

Keeping Your Covenant is a life-changing tool that is fun and easy to use. We invite you to lead a small group through this introductory study to the HomeBuilders Couples Series®. You'll find the material to be practical, thought-provoking, and refreshing.

Some friends of ours, Roy and Susan Milam, have been true difference-makers in their community. Roy recalled: "A friend challenged me with words I'll never forget: 'Life is not a dress rehearsal. If you really want to make a difference in this world, maybe you ought to think about leading a HomeBuilders.'"

Roy explained that he and his wife saw their marriage and others' marriages transformed as they led their first group: "Husbands and wives began communicating about issues they had never discussed. Couples who were angry and resentful became supportive and loving. We saw God work in lots of wonderful ways through HomeBuilders."

Like the Milams, you, too, can reach out to our hurting world. As you spend four evenings leading *Keeping Your Covenant*, you will be encouraged and challenged as you make new friends and strengthen your own marriage. After all, there are only a "few hours before sunset."

Yours for godly homes,

Dennis & Barbara

Dennis and Barbara Rainey

Keeping Your Covenant

A Small-Group Study to Enrich Your Marriage

A reproducible introductory study to
the HomeBuilders Couples Series®

Little Rock, Arkansas

Keeping Your Covenant: A Small-Group Study to Enrich Your Marriage
© 1999 by FamilyLife. All rights reserved.
Published by FamilyLife, a division of Campus Crusade for Christ.

Designed by Claes Jonasson
Edited by Mary Larmoyeux
Contributors: Dave Boehi, Ben Colter, Drew and Kit Coons

Printed in the United States of America.
ISBN: 1-57229-1915

Sessions adapted from HomeBuilders Couples Series® by permission. Reproducible only in the format contained in this booklet. All HomeBuilders Couples Series® study and leader's guides are copyrighted materials and may not be reproduced. The only exception is the HomeBuilders Couples Series® Bible Study Elective curriculum for churches.

Except where noted, Scriptures are taken from the New American Standard Bible®. © 1960, 1962, 1963, 1968, 1971, 1972, 1973, 1975, 1977, 1994 by The Lockman Foundation. Used by permission.

Scripture references used in "The Four Spiritual Laws" excerpt (in Appendix A of this book) are taken from the Holy Bible, New International Version®. Copyright © 1973, 1978, 1984 by International Bible Society. Used by permission of Zondervan Publishing House. All rights reserved. The "NIV" and "New International Version" trademarks are registered in the United States Patent and Trademark Office by International Bible Society. Use of either trademark requires the permission of International Bible Society.

FamilyLife
3900 N. Rodney Parham Rd.
Little Rock, AR 72212-2441
(501) 223-8663
1-800-FL-TODAY
www.familylife.com

Dennis Rainey, Executive Director

A division of Campus Crusade for Christ

Table of Contents

Before You Begin 7

Getting Additional Copies of This Booklet 8

Session One 9

I Take You: Receiving Your Mate
(Adapted by permission from *Building Your Marriage* by Dennis Rainey)

Session Two 15

To Be Your Husband/Wife: Comprehending Your Mate's Differentness
(Adapted by permission from *Building Teamwork in Your Marriage* by Robert Lewis)

Session Three 21

Love, Honor, and Cherish: Planting Positive Words
(Adapted by permission from *Building Your Mate's Self-Esteem* by Dennis and Barbara Rainey)

Session Four 27

To Have and to Hold: The Power of Prayer in Your Marriage
(Adapted by permission from *Growing Together in Christ* by David Sunde)

Conclusion 35

Where Do We Go From Here?
Description of FamilyLife Resources

Appendix A 39

The Four Spiritual Laws

Appendix B—Leader's Tips 45

Who Can Lead HomeBuilders?
Starting a HomeBuilders Group
Leading a HomeBuilders Group
Most Commonly Asked Questions

Appendix C 53

Leader's Notes (answers to Sessions One - Four)

Appendix D 63

Tear-Out Order Form and Evaluation

BEFORE YOU BEGIN

Congratulations on deciding to invest your time and energy into your marriage. You will experience life-change through the biblical truths found in *Keeping Your Covenant*, develop lasting friendships, and be encouraged as you interact with other couples. May God bless you on your new journey!

NOTES TO GROUP LEADERS

How to Get Started: The most important thing you can do is pray. Ask God to motivate and equip you to strengthen your marriage and help others.

Your introductory study, *Keeping Your Covenant*, may be photocopied for a group if you wish to do so (additional copies can also be purchased from FamilyLife). The study has been adapted from four existing HomeBuilders studies to give you a sampling of different topics available to your group.

Appendix B contains some helpful information on facilitating small groups. You will find:

- Starting a HomeBuilders group
- Childcare
- The most commonly asked questions
- And much more

How to Lead: As you will soon learn, leading a HomeBuilders group does not require an expert Bible teacher or even a couple with a "good" marriage. You are to be a facilitator who provides an open, warm environment where couples accept one another.

You will want to review the leader's notes before each session in Appendix C. There are only three ground rules for HomeBuilders group members:

- Share nothing that will embarrass your mate.
- You may pass on any question.
- Complete the project with your mate prior to each session.

It is important to start and end your sessions on time. Also, couples need to be committed to completing all four sessions and each of the HomeBuilders Projects.

How to Keep Going: After you complete *Keeping Your Covenant*, encourage your group to choose another HomeBuilders study. Refer to the Conclusion section of this booklet for some helpful information.

GETTING ADDITIONAL COPIES OF THIS BOOKLET

We encourage you to get a group together to study *Keeping Your Covenant*. You may photocopy this booklet or download the text from our Web site at www.familylife.com; however, we ask that you do so **only** under the following conditions:

- You are using the copies for a noncommercial purpose.
- You will not use this material in (or on) a product for sale.
- You will not sell the copies.

Additional *Keeping Your Covenant* booklets are available from FamilyLife at $4.95 each. To place your order, you may call 1-800-FL-TODAY or use the order form at the back of this booklet.

Session One

I TAKE YOU: RECEIVING YOUR MATE

Oneness in marriage requires receiving your mate as God's perfect provision for your needs.

(10-15 minutes)

Introduce yourselves as a couple by telling the group the three following things about your relationship (you might want to talk briefly with each other to decide what to tell the group):

- Where and when you met (be sure to make this brief!)

- One fun or unique date before your marriage

- One humorous or romantic time from your honeymoon or early married life

(to be done as a group—45-50 minutes)

A Cause of Failure in Marriage

1. During engagement and early marriage, many couples seem to experience a high level of romance and emotional closeness. But as time goes by their relationship may slowly become more distant. Why do you think this is so?

2. Read Jesus' story in Matthew 7:24-27.

- What does this parable teach us?

- How does it relate to building a strong marriage?

Building From God's Plan

Read Genesis 2:18-23 where we find the familiar story of Adam and Eve. Our familiarity with Scriptures such as this can blind us to profound insights—insights that, when applied, can strengthen every marriage. Let's look at what we can learn from this passage to help us achieve unity in marriage.

3. What need did God build into Adam that was not filled by God's personal presence? What was "not good" about Adam as God created him?

4. What are some likely reasons why God made Adam incomplete?

5. After God declared it was not good for Adam to be alone, His next step was to create animals and birds and bring them to Adam so he could name them. What did naming animals have to do with Adam's aloneness?

6. What are some ways you see your need for your mate today that you did not recognize when you first got married?

7. Read Genesis 2:21-22. This passage indicates God did five things to create Eve:

- He caused Adam to sleep.
- He took one of Adam's ribs.
- He created a woman from the rib.
- He closed Adam's flesh.
- He brought Eve to Adam.

Which of these actions seems most significant to you? Why?

8. At the beginning of your relationship with your mate, how aware was God of all your needs (past, present, and future)?

Our Response to God's Provision

Read Genesis 2:23

9. Why was Adam able to immediately recognize Eve as the mate who would fulfill his need?

10. What causes us to reject rather than receive our mate?

11. Since God provided your mate, can you reject your mate without rejecting God? Why?

12. Individually, list ways you see your mate needing you. (Try to list five if time permits.) Share your list with your mate.

Make a date with your mate to meet in the next few days to complete **HomeBuilders Project #1**. Your leader will ask at the next session for you to share one thing from this experience.

____________	____________	______________________________
Date	Time	Location

Individually: 25 minutes

1. Review the material covered during Session One. What concepts made the biggest impression on you?

2. Do an inventory of the ways your mate is meeting your needs. Try to list 25 or more if you can. (List on a separate sheet of paper.)

3. Identify which of those are the five most important ways you need him or her.

4. Identify those differences in your mate that God uses to complete you.

5. Identify one or two areas in which you may have been rejecting or not totally accepting your mate. What has been the result of that rejection for you? For your mate?

6. Do you need to ask forgiveness for your lack of acceptance toward your mate? If appropriate, express this to your mate.

Interact as a Couple: 15-20 minutes

1. Share your answers from the individual section with your mate.

2. Affirm (or reaffirm) to your mate your acceptance of him or her as God's perfect provision for your needs.

3. Close your time together in prayer, thanking God for one another.

Session Two

TO BE YOUR HUSBAND/WIFE: COMPREHENDING YOUR MATE'S DIFFERENTNESS

Men and women are more than noticeably different. Understanding and responding to these deeper differences is vital to building a good marriage.

(10-15 minutes)

1. What is one important thing you learned as you completed **HomeBuilders Project #1?**

◆ Complete the following statement: "My marriage has taught me some important things about the opposite sex. For example, ..."

(to be done as a group—45-50 minutes)

And God created man in His own image, in the image of God He created him; male and female He created them. Genesis 1:27

God did a wonderful thing when He divided man into "male and female." He called His two creations "very good" (Genesis 1:31). The differences separating man as male and woman as female were intended to usher in many special blessings (Genesis 1:28). Unfortunately, with the fall of man, the blessings of the sexes became more a battle between the sexes. The unique qualities with which God endowed each gender now gave rise to misunderstanding and contention rather than completion and power.

Becoming a student of the opposite sex is a great starting place for building a good marriage (or rebuilding a damaged one).

Practical Differences

1. Below are a series of general observations social scientists have made regarding male and female differences. Discuss with your group how each of these differences has at times manifested itself in your marriage. What misunderstandings (if any) have resulted because of them? (Remember, these are general observations, not scientific facts.)

◆ Women have a greater need of belonging; men have a greater need of achieving.

- Women are more sensitive than men; the expressing of feelings is more important to them.

- Men tend to see their work as extensions of themselves; women are apt to see their husbands and families that way.

- Men are more goal-oriented; women more need-oriented.

- Men are more focused in their thinking; women are more intuitive in their thinking.

- Women tend to require more frequent reassurance.

- Men are more physical; women are more relational.

A Call to Understanding

God never intended for male and female differences to divide husbands and wives or bring conflict between them. Quite the contrary; God's original intent was for us to appreciate and honor those unique qualities which our mate possesses. The Scripture appeals to us to adopt this kind of perspective.

2. Read 1 Peter 3:7. What are the two major exhortations to husbands in this passage?

-

-

3. How does the first exhortation in this passage call for a recognition of the differences between the sexes?

4. The key word to living successfully with the opposite sex is the word, "understanding." Practically, how do you think one goes about obtaining this understanding? What's the process?

5. Contrast the "understanding way" being called for by Peter in 1 Peter 3:7 (i.e., the Scripture) with the "way" of Proverbs 16:25 (the way that so many choose in living with their mates). What is this other "way"? Explain.

6. Now notice the second exhortation within 1 Peter 3:7. What major social movement has resulted in part because men have trusted in their natural instincts rather than "the way" encouraged by this Scripture verse?

7. Despite their differences, what "status" does Peter say a husband must always be reaffirming in his wife?

8. What are some practical ways a husband can do this?

9. Share with your mate the areas of your marriage that come to mind as a result of tonight's discussion.

Make a date with your mate to meet in the next few days to complete **HomeBuilders Project #2.** You will be asked to share one thing from this experience when you meet for Session Three.

Date	Time	Location

Individually: 10 minutes

1. List one thing you want your mate to understand about you that you feel he (or she) is unaware of because of your gender difference.

2. List one thing you are having difficulty with in understanding your mate.

3. In what area has this affected the quality of your marriage?

4. How can you communicate about this in a way that does not attack your mate but instead gives insight and understanding.

Interact as a Couple: 30 minutes

Read together Ephesians 4:29-32 before beginning your interaction to set the tone of your discussion.

1. Share with your mate your answers to the previous questions. (Listen carefully and seek to understand your mate's differentness.)

2. Commit to a plan of action that will honor your mate in regard to the things that have been communicated to you. Write out your action plan below. Remember, understanding and responding to male and female differences is important to building a good marriage.

Session Three

Love, Honor, and Cherish: Planting Positive Words

The words you speak to your mate have the potential to strengthen or poison your mate's self-esteem.

(10 minutes)

Begin this session by sharing one thing you learned from **HomeBuilders Project #2.**

List four or five of the most descriptive words or phrases about yourself on a sheet of paper. Your leader will randomly read these out loud and everyone will guess who is being described.

(to be done as a group—35 minutes)

The Power of Words

1. "Sticks and stones may break my bones, but words will never hurt me." We're familiar with this childhood saying. Comment on the accuracy or inaccuracy of this saying as you see it as an adult.

2. Think back on the power of words in your life. While growing up, what were some statements made about you that you can still remember? Who said them? (Try to think of positive words as well as negative words. Which category is easier to remember? Why?) What effects did these words have on you?

3. Now let's look into the Scriptures and see how the power of words is described.

- Proverbs 11:9
- Proverbs 12:25
- Ephesians 4:29

4. If possible, recall some of the words you used to affirm your mate during your courtship. What was the effect of those words upon your mate, your relationship, and you?

5. After having been married for a while, why is there a tendency to become callous or insensitive to the effects that words have on your mate? How can understanding the power of words begin to change your vocabulary with your mate?

Since words must be used carefully and constructively in building self-esteem, let's consider how best to speak rightly to your mate.

The Power of Praise

6. Why do many people find it difficult to give or receive praise?

7. For what character qualities can you give your mate praise?

8. It is important to praise your mate specifically. After finishing the following statements, share them with your mate.

- Thank you for…
- You made me feel loved when…

- I like being with you because...

- I think you're growing in...

9. For your mate's praise to be effective, wise, and truthful you need to communicate when and how best to praise you. Share with the group when you most need to be praised. What's the best method for your mate to use with you (letter, note, hug, phone call, etc.)?

10. It is important that you be generous in praising your mate. The following are three areas where you can be generous in praise: encouragement, appreciation, and expressing belief in your mate. What type of statements—

- encourage you?

- communicate you are appreciated?

- express belief to you?

11. Read Ephesians 4:29. Then, while thinking of the earlier discussion on praise, share one practical application that you can use for your own marriage.

Conclude this time in prayer, thanking God for the praiseworthy qualities of your mate.

Make a date with your mate to meet in the next few days to complete **HomeBuilders Project #3**. You will be asked to share one thing from this experience when you meet for Session Four.

Date	Time	Location

Individually: 30 minutes

1. List some words and phrases that you plant in your mate's life that produce:

- weeds

- fruit

2. Are there any "weed seeds" you have planted in your mate's life for which you need to ask forgiveness?

3. What are some words or phrases that discourage you?

4. What are some words or phrases that encourage you?

5. Complete the following sentences:

- My mate can express belief in me by _______.
- If I am discouraged, my mate can encourage me by ______.

6. Write a paragraph or a letter to your mate expressing praise, appreciation, encouragement, or belief in your mate. (Please express your unconditional love and be specific—avoid generalities.)

Interact as a Couple: 30 minutes

1. Share your answers from the individual time.

Session Four

To Have and to Hold: The Power of Prayer in Your Marriage

Prayer promotes growth both in your relationship with God and in your relationship with your mate.

(10 minutes)

Whether or not you grew up in a Christian home, you learned something about prayer as you grew up and observed the attitudes and practices of family, friends, church members, or even characters in television shows and movies.

- What kinds of prayers did you pray as a child?

- What do you think you learned about prayer when you were a child?

(25 minutes)

Prayer Barriers and Benefits

1. What do you think the average Christian thinks about prayer? What keeps people from praying more than they do?

2. Why do you think Christian couples often fail to spend much time together in prayer?

3. How do most men feel about praying with their wives? How do most wives feel about praying with their husbands?

4. What do the following verses tell you about how prayer will help you grow in your relationship with God?

- John 16:24

- James 1:5

5. Read 1 John 5:14-15. Why do you think God wants us to ask Him to answer specific requests?

6. If you can, share how you've seen God answer a specific prayer request.

Basic Components of Prayer

Because prayer is talking with God, it's a wonderful way to develop your relationship with Him. But many people know little about what to do as they pray.

The psalms of the Bible are among the best-known and best-loved writings of all literature. Many psalms are actually prayers, and from them we can learn about some basic components of prayer.

7. Psalm 96 illustrates one major component of prayer: praise of God. "Praising God" means focusing on His character and His deeds and giving Him public acclaim. Read verses 1-10.

- If you were to spend time consistently praising God like this, how would that practice affect the way you look at various problems you encounter in life?

- What is something you can praise God for right now?

8. Psalm 51 is treasured as one of the greatest expressions of confession. Read verses 1-13, in which King David confesses his transgressions (committing adultery with Bathsheba and sending her husband off to be killed in battle).

- How would you describe the burden David felt because of his sin?

- What did David's confession accomplish?

- What would happen in a marriage relationship if one partner was not confessing sin to God?

9. Read 1 John 1:9. What happens when you confess a specific sin?

10. Psalm 34 is often read and quoted to encourage us to bring our needs and desires to God in prayer. This third component of prayer is called supplication. Read verses 4-18. What do you find in these verses that would motivate you to pray regularly?

11. As a couple, discuss together how your marriage would benefit if you were to pray together regularly as a couple. If you do pray regularly as a couple, what can you do to make prayer exciting?

12. What does Matthew 7:7-11 have to say about making requests to the Lord?

What's Next?

Now that you know what HomeBuilders is all about, why not continue?

Read through the Conclusion section (beginning on page 35) for a complete description of the entire HomeBuilders Couples Series. If you have gone through this booklet in a group setting, you may want to discuss your next steps with your group. However, if you and your spouse have completed it as a couple, consider joining or leading a HomeBuilders group yourself.

Make a Date

Make a date with your mate to meet in the next few days to complete **HomeBuilders Project #4**. This project will help you as a couple in developing a more consistent prayer life.

____________	____________	______________________________
Date	Time	Location

Individually: 30 minutes

1. Why do many Christians spend most of their prayer time asking God to grant their requests while devoting little time to praising God or confessing sins? Why are praise and confession so important if we are to grow in Christ?

2. When you pray, on which of the three components (praise, confession, supplication) do you spend the most time? On which do you spend the least amount of time?

3. Of the three components, what would be most difficult for you to do together as a couple? Why do you think it's important for you to include that component in your prayer together?

4. Using Psalm 96 as a guide, spend some time praising God for who He is and what He has done in your life. Write a list of specific things to praise Him for.

5. Read 1 John 1:9 again. Spend a few moments confessing any sin that is blocking growth in your relationship with God. Then thank Him for forgiving those sins.

Suggestion: Write down your sins on a sheet of paper, then write "1 John 1:9" across the list. To demonstrate your faith that God has kept His promise to "cleanse us from all unrighteousness" when we confess our sins, tear the paper up, and throw it away.

6. What are some needs in your life at this time? List them below as prayer requests, then spend some time praying through the list.

7. What are some needs in your mate's life? List them below as prayer requests, then spend some time praying through the list.

Interact as a Couple: 30 minutes

1. Share with each other the insights from your individual time.

2. What motivates the two of you to pray together?

3. What do you think would be the best time and place for prayer together?

4. Spend a few minutes in prayer together, following the outline of praise, confession, and supplication.

5. Fill in the blanks of the following commitment form, and sign the pledge on your sheet and your partner's.

"We agree that we will pray together

at ______________________________ (time and place)."

______________________________ (signed) ______________ (date)

______________________________ (signed) ______________ (date)

CONCLUSION

Where Do We Go From Here?

You have been working on the most important commitment of your life—spending time with God and with your spouse. You are probably asking yourselves, "Where do we go from here?"

If your group decides to do another study together, you'll be excited to know that FamilyLife's HomeBuilders Couples Series® is a collection of nine exciting small-group studies.

As a group, decide:

- When will we begin a new study? ____________________
- What study will we use? ____________________
- Who will facilitate it? ____________________
- Where will we meet? ____________________
- Who will order the materials? ____________________

Investing in your marriage will help you keep it strong, dynamic, and solid—able to withstand the storms of life.

FamilyLife Resources

Almost one million people have used the HomeBuilders Couples Series® to help strengthen and build their relationships on the solid biblical principles found in God's Word. Designed by FamilyLife for small groups of four to seven couples, the individual studies cover a variety of marriage issues and contain six to eight sessions in a spiral bound format for easy use.

Each member of the group is encouraged to have his or her own study guide. A separate leader's guide with notes and helpful tips is also available.

All HomeBuilders Couples Series® study and leader's guides are copyrighted materials and may not be reproduced. The only exception is the HomeBuilders Couples Series® Bible Study Elective curriculum for churches.

Ideal for New Groups

*Building Your Marriage**
by Dennis Rainey
Discover and apply God's basic blueprints for a strong, healthy marriage that will last a lifetime. (7 sessions)

*Building Teamwork in Your Marriage**
by Robert Lewis
Understand your differences are gifts from God, and learn how you are the unique person equipped to complete your mate! (7 sessions)

*Growing Together in Christ**
by David Sunde
Discover the power and joy you and your mate can find together by developing an exciting, daily relationship with Christ. (6 sessions)

Great for Outreach or Specific Needs

Resolving Conflict in Your Marriage
by Bob and Jan Horner
Every marriage has its share of conflict. Learn to transform conflicts into opportunities to energize your marriage and increase your love for your mate. (6 sessions)

Mastering Money in Your Marriage
by Ron Blue
You can learn how to manage money wisely regardless of your income level. Through this study, you can put your finances under God's control. Discover how you can make money matters a tool for growth instead of a bone of contention in your marriage. (7 sessions)

Managing Pressure in Your Marriage
by Dennis Rainey and Robert Lewis
This study will help you manage stress and eliminate needless pressure. Learn to make better choices and plan for the future. (6 sessions)

For Experienced Groups

*Building Your Mate's Self-Esteem**
by Dennis and Barbara Rainey
Improve your marriage by learning how to encourage your mate. Experience new levels of love and fulfillment. (8 sessions)

Life Choices for a Lasting Marriage
by David Boehi
How can you keep your marriage strong against a hostile culture? As a couple, learn how to deal with temptation, simplify your lifestyle, and renew your minds with the truth of God's Word. (6 sessions)

Expressing Love in Your Marriage
by Jerry and Sheryl Wunder, Dennis and Jill Eenigenburg
Begin setting aside the false ideas of love promoted by our culture. Learn to express God's love in your marriage—not a fleeting emotion but a divinely inspired commitment. (6 sessions)

Additional HomeBuilders Resources

Preparing for Marriage
by David Boehi, Brent Nelson, Jeff Schulte, and Lloyd Shadrach
This study includes six fun, romantic sessions and five special projects that will prepare couples for loving, lasting marriages firmly established in Jesus Christ. To get the most from this study, each person will need a copy of *Preparing for Marriage.*

Leader's Guide: Preparing for Marriage
by David Boehi, Brent Nelson, Jeff Schulte, and Lloyd Shadrach
This leader's guide is a supplement to *Preparing for Marriage.* It is an invaluable tool for pastors, Christian marriage counselors, and mentor couples to help engaged couples build from the bloom of new romance a vision of a lasting marriage firmly established in Jesus Christ.

Orientation Manual: An Introduction to HomeBuilders
This 47-page booklet will equip you to be a difference-maker by leading a HomeBuilders study. It contains one sample HomeBuilders session, tips for starting a group, and a helpful listing of resources.

New studies are under development—on topics including parenting adolescents and blended families.

To order HomeBuilders resources:

See order form at the back of this booklet, or

- Call 1-800-FL-TODAY
- Visit our Web site: www.familylife.com
- Visit your local Christian bookstore where most studies are available

*Available in Bible study elective format for Sunday school.

APPENDIX A

THE FOUR SPIRITUAL LAWS*

Draw closer to God and you will be able to draw closer to your mate. Here's how you can begin a personal relationship with God . . .

Just as there are physical laws that govern the physical universe, so are there spiritual laws that govern your relationship with God.

LAW 1	God **loves** you and offers a wonderful **plan** for your life.

God's Love

"For God so loved the world that He gave His one and only Son, that whoever believes in Him shall not perish but have eternal life" (John 3:16, NIV).

God's Plan

[Christ speaking] "I came that they might have life, and might have it abundantly" [that it might be full and meaningful] (John 10:10).

Why is it that most people are not experiencing the abundant life? Because. . .

LAW 2 **Man is sinful and separated from God. Therefore, he cannot know and experience God's love and plan for his life.**

Man Is Sinful

"All have sinned and fall short of the glory of God" (Romans 3:23).

Man was created to have fellowship with God; but, because of his stubborn self-will, chose to go his own independent way, and fellowship with God was broken. This self-will, characterized by an attitude of active rebellion or passive indifference, is evidence of what the Bible calls sin.

Man Is Separated

"The wages of sin is death" [spiritual separation from God] (Romans 6:23).

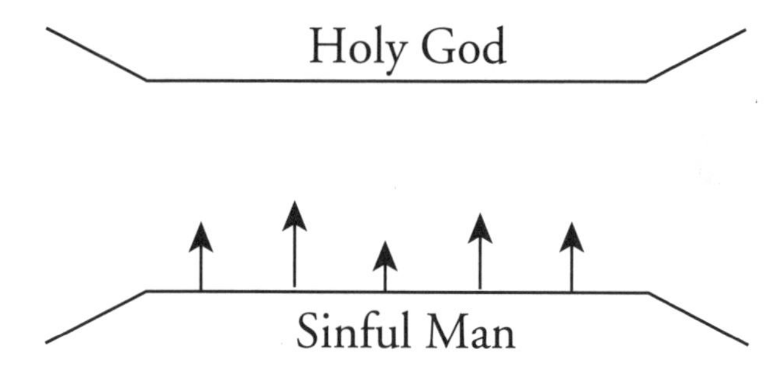

This diagram illustrates that God is holy and man is sinful. A great gulf separates the two. The arrows illustrate that man is continually trying to reach God and the abundant life through his own efforts, such as a good life, philosophy, or religion—but he inevitably fails.

The third law explains the only way to bridge this gulf . . .

LAW 3	**Jesus Christ is God's only provision for man's sin. Through Him you can know and experience God's love and plan for your life.**

He Died in Our Place

"God demonstrates His own love toward us, in that while we were yet sinners, Christ died for us" (Romans 5:8).

He Rose From the Dead

"Christ died for our sins . . . He was buried . . . He was raised on the third day according to the Scriptures . . . He appeared to Peter, then to the twelve. After that He appeared to more than five hundred . . ."
(1 Corinthians 15:3-6).

He Is the Only Way to God

"Jesus said to him, 'I am the way, and the truth, and the life; no one comes to the Father, but through Me'" (John 14:6).

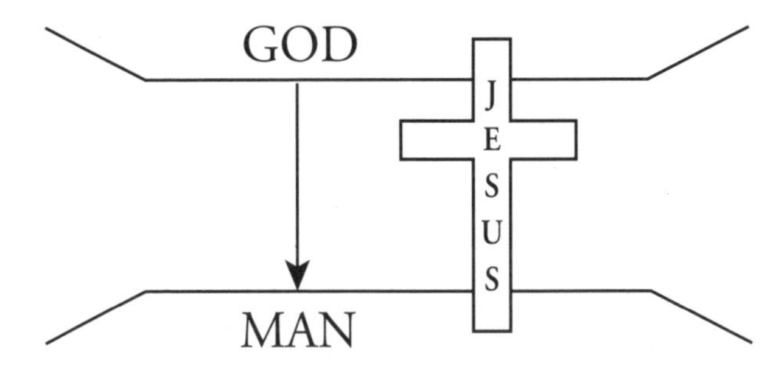

This diagram illustrates that God has bridged the gulf that separates us from Him by sending His Son, Jesus Christ, to die on the cross in our place to pay the penalty for our sins.

It is not enough just to know these three laws . . .

LAW 4	**We must individually receive Jesus Christ as Savior and Lord; then we can know and experience God's love and plan for our lives.**

We Must Receive Christ

"As many as received Him, to them He gave the right to become children of God, even to those who believe in His name" (John 1:12).

We Receive Christ Through Faith

"By grace you have been saved through faith; and that not of yourselves, it is the gift of God; not as a result of works, that no one should boast" (Ephesians 2:8,9).

When We Receive Christ, We Experience a New Birth

(Read John 3:1-8.)

We Receive Christ Through Personal Invitation

[Christ is speaking] "Behold, I stand at the door and knock; if any one hears My voice and opens the door, I will come in to him" (Revelation 3:20).

Receiving Christ involves turning to God from self (repentance) and trusting Christ to come into our lives to forgive our sins and to make us what He wants us to be. Just to agree **intellectually** that Jesus Christ is the Son of God and that He died on the cross for our sins is not enough. Nor is it enough to have an **emotional** experience. We receive Jesus Christ by **faith**, as an act of the **will**.

These two circles represent two kinds of lives:

Self-Directed Life

S – Self is on the throne
† – Christ is outside the life
• – Interests are directed by self, often resulting in discord and frustration

Christ-Directed Life

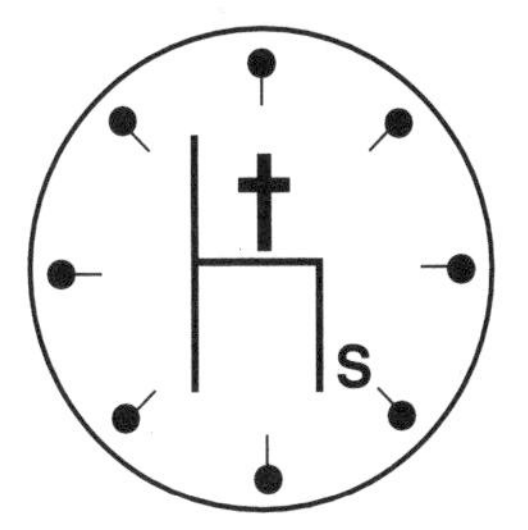

† – Christ is in the life and on the throne
S – Self is yielding to Christ
• – Interests are directed by Christ, resulting in harmony with God's plan

Which circle best represents your life?
Which circle would you like to have represent your life?

The following explains how you can receive Christ:

You Can Receive Christ Right Now By Faith Through Prayer

(Prayer is talking with God.)

God knows your heart and is not so concerned with your words as He is with the attitude of your heart. The following is a suggested prayer:

"Lord Jesus, I need You. Thank You for dying on the cross for my sins. I open the door of my life and receive You as my Savior and Lord. Thank You for forgiving my sins and giving me eternal life. Take control of the throne of my life. Make me the kind of person You want me to be."

Does this prayer express the desire of your heart?

If it does, I invite you to pray this prayer right now, and Christ will come into your life, as He promised.

Fellowship in a Good Church

God's Word instructs us not to forsake "the assembling of ourselves together" (Hebrews 10:25). Several logs burn brightly together, but put one aside on the cold hearth and the fire goes out. So it is with your relationship with other Christians.

If you do not belong to a church, do not wait to be invited. Take the initiative; call the pastor of a nearby church where Christ is honored and His Word is preached. Start this week, and make plans to attend regularly.

*Written by Bill Bright. Copyright ©1965, 1994 Campus Crusade for Christ, Inc., all rights reserved.

If you have come to know Christ personally through this presentation of the gospel, write or call FamilyLife for a free packet of materials especially prepared to assist you in your Christian growth. A special Bible study series and an abundance of other helpful materials for Christian growth are also available.

FamilyLife
P.O. Box 8220
Little Rock, AR 72221-8220
1-800-FL-TODAY
www.familylife.com

APPENDIX B

LEADER'S TIPS

Who Can Lead HomeBuilders?

Leading a HomeBuilders group does not require an expert Bible teacher or even a couple with a "good" marriage. The group is led by a facilitator, not a lecturer. The main function of the facilitator is to provide an environment of openness, warmth, and acceptance of one another.

The facilitator is a fellow member of the group who has the added responsibility of guiding the group in the right direction within the limited time period. The best leaders are couples who are willing to share their successes and weaknesses while trying to have a better marriage.

If you are unsure about your ability to lead, consider co-leading with another couple. You can divide the responsibilities. Together you can trust God to work in your lives and help other couples.

By leading a HomeBuilders group you will:

- Invest in your own marriage
- Study the Bible
- Grow in Christian character
- Have fun, make friends, and deepen friendships
- Serve your church
- Do your children a favor by strengthening your family
- Make a difference in the lives of others

Starting a HomeBuilders Group

As a couple, commit to each other and to God to make the HomeBuilders group a priority for the time it will take to complete the study. (Remember, it only requires a short-term commitment. You may choose to meet weekly or every other week.) Decide how you will share responsibility for organizing and leading the group, preparing for the session, phone calling, and details of hospitality.

Inviting Couples to Participate in a Neighborhood Group

Consider asking the couples who attended a FamilyLife Conference or an "I Still Do™" event with you. You may also want to invite your friends, neighbors, co-workers, couples from church, and parents from PTA or your children's sports. A personal invitation is always best when you tell how much a FamilyLife Conference, "I Still Do" event, or other FamilyLife outreach has meant to you.

Show potential group members the materials and tell them about the discussion format. You will want to assure couples that the study will help make a good marriage better, and that they will be making a limited time commitment.

You may want to host a small event to arouse interest in HomeBuilders. A neighborhood cookout or potluck can be an excellent occasion to introduce others to HomeBuilders. A romantic dinner party at a restaurant or hotel with a short biblical message on marriage is another good way to get couples interested. (Be sure and tell couples about the topic of the message when you are inviting them.)

Starting HomeBuilders in Your Church

If you are interested in starting HomeBuilders in your church, volunteer to lead a group there. Make it clear to your pastor that you will do the work, and show him the HomeBuilders promotional and study material. (Contact FamilyLife for other available HomeBuilders information.) Explain how the principles from the study have affected your life, and share how churches can use HomeBuilders in a variety of ways. But, if the pastor is not interested, respect his wishes and start a neighborhood group.

Small Groups—Churches most frequently use HomeBuilders in small groups or as an evening Bible study. If small groups already exist at your church, talk with the person who makes decisions on the curriculum. If there are no small groups currently meeting, you could offer to organize a "pilot project" and begin with one or two groups.

Retreats or Weekend Emphasis—A church or Sunday school class often sets aside a weekend to emphasize strong marriages. This provides a great setting to share a series of HomeBuilders sessions.

Sunday School—Four HomeBuilders studies have been adapted specifically for the Sunday school class setting: *Building Teamwork in Your Marriage, Building Your Marriage, Building Your Mate's Self-Esteem*, and *Growing Together in Christ*. See the order form at the back of this booklet, or contact FamilyLife at 1-800-FL-TODAY or www.familylife.com. You can also pick up these resources at your local Christian bookstore.

Church Promotion—Consider the following ideas:
- Send invitations to church members and neighbors.
- Advertise in the church bulletin, newsletter, or flyers.
- Conduct an introductory meeting to demonstrate the effectiveness and fun of HomeBuilders.
- Have your pastor endorse HomeBuilders from the pulpit.
- Use sign-up sheets.
- Invite your pastor or couples' Sunday school teachers to observe an existing class.

Childcare

It is important that your group focus on the study material without distractions and interruptions. Ask your group what works best for them. Childcare must be dependable. Some couples will not be able to commit to every group session if childcare is not provided. Here are some suggestions:
- Arrange babysitting in one house and hold the study in another.
- Pool resources to hire a babysitter.
- Contact your youth pastor for referrals.
- Ask if any couples have older children who would babysit.
- Use available childcare or church facilities when the nursery is open.

Leading a HomeBuilders Group

Before you begin each session, agree as a couple how much you will communicate about your own marriage. Sharing openly will help others apply the biblical truths to their lives. Study the leader's notes in Appendix C and pray regularly for your group. Also, discuss as a couple leadership responsibilities for each session.

It is also important to practice hospitality. Making friends is a key to creating an environment in which God will change lives. In our impersonal world, many couples are hungry for friendships. God will use your relationships in an atmosphere of mild accountability to encourage couples to apply the lessons to their lives.

Starting the Session

It is important to start on time. Share the following ground rules at the beginning of the first session, and review them as needed:

- Share nothing about your marriage which will embarrass your mate. Your mate is the best judge about what is appropriate.
- You may "pass" on any question you do not want to answer. Nobody is forced to say anything.
- Each couple should complete the **HomeBuilders Projects** (questions for each couple to discuss and act on) between each session.

The Session Itself

Simply read through the questions to lead the study. At first, you may need to wait for answers. Don't jump in too quickly with your own ideas, couples will wait for you and you will end up teaching the material. Ideas you can solicit from the group will mean more to the participants than those you "teach." When discussion is going too long or gets off the subject, just read the next question to stay on track.

Wrapping Up

Plan your time and watch the clock to keep the session moving. It is always best to end on time—sending couples away wanting more, rather than exhausted. And of course, you should have social time or a dessert afterwards. The couples who need to leave can do so, and others can stay longer. Emphasize the **HomeBuilders Project** just before the session ends.

Most Commonly Asked Questions

1. Who should participate?

The concepts in this study will benefit any couple, whether they are newlyweds, engaged, or have been married for many years.

2. How many couples should be in this study group?

Ideally, four to seven couples (including you and your mate). While a positive response may be greater among those who know you, consider asking acquaintances, neighbors, and work associates. (Four of the HomeBuilders Couples Series studies are available in Bible study elective format which is ideal for a large-group study at church.)

3. What if one partner does not want to participate?

Expect that some people will attend the first session wishing that they were somewhere else. You can dispel a great deal of anxiety and resistance at the first session by mentioning that you know that there are probably some who came reluctantly. Mention that you are pleased that each person is there regardless of why anyone has come.

Briefly comment that you are confident that each person will enjoy the study and will benefit from it. Mention that the commitment to *Keeping Your Covenant* is short-term (only four sessions) and that the potential benefits could last a lifetime. Also, assure the group that at no time will anyone be forced to share publicly.

4. Should an individual join the group alone?

It is best if a person does not join HomeBuilders alone. Learning the principles and seeing everyone else working together on their marriages would cause discouragement and dissatisfaction with the individual's spouse. This does not mean if a person's spouse is out of town, perhaps on business, that they should skip the study. If their spouse is a regular member, they should attend.

5. Can a non-Christian participate in this study?

Although the study is targeted for Christians, non-Christian couples could participate in it. Welcome the non-Christian into your group and seek to get to know the person during the early weeks of the study. Sometime during the study, schedule a time to meet with this person or couple privately to explain the principles on which this study is built. Share about Christ and offer an opportunity to receive Him as Savior and Lord. We recommend "The Four Spiritual Laws" to help you explain how a person can know God. (This information is found in Appendix A of this booklet.) Many men and women have come to know Jesus Christ through the HomeBuilders Couples Series.

6. What is the best setting for a group meeting?
In general, inviting couples to your home provides a friendly atmosphere. You need to have a place where everyone can sit comfortably and see and hear each other. If your home will not work, see if another couple in the group would be willing to host the sessions while you lead them.

7. What time schedule should we follow?
Allow one hour for each session—but remember, this doesn't include time for fellowship or refreshments.

8. What are the ground rules for the study?

- Share nothing that will embarrass your mate.
- You may pass on any question.
- Complete the project with your mate prior to each session.

9. What other things are important to communicate to the group?
It is important that the couples commit to the group, to each other, and to the process of developing oneness in their marriages. They should also be committed to coming to each of the four sessions.

10. After introducing HomeBuilders, what should the group decide?

- Meeting nights and times
- Where to meet
- Who will be responsible for refreshments (This is good to rotate after the first meeting.)
- If needed, babysitting arrangements

11. What is the group leader's responsibility?
It is critical that you assume the role of facilitator. Help the group interact and discuss the information. Be careful not to lecture or allow the group to ramble aimlessly. Guide the group using the leader's tips and notes at the back of this booklet. Strongly encourage group members to complete every project—by doing so they will get the most from the sessions. Commit to pray regularly for the couples in your group.

12. Do you have suggestions about facilitating the group discussion?
Keep the focus on what Scripture says. When someone disagrees with Scripture, affirm him or her for wrestling with the issue and point out that some biblical statements are hard to understand or to accept. Encourage the person to keep an open mind on the issue at least

through the remainder of the sessions.

Avoid labeling an answer as "wrong"; doing so can kill the atmosphere for discussion. Encourage a person who gives a wrong or incomplete answer to look again at the question or the Scripture being explored. Offer a comment such as, "That's really close" or "There's something else we need to see there." Or ask others in the group to respond.

13. How can I get everyone to participate in group discussion?

◆ Rather than pose a question, ask non-participators to share an opinion or a personal experience.
◆ The overly talkative person can be kept in control by the use of devices that call for responses in a specific manner:

> "I'd like this question to be answered first by the husband of the couple with the next anniversary."
>
> "...the wife of the couple who had the shortest engagement."
>
> "...anyone who complained about doing the project from the last session."

14. How much should we communicate about our own marriage?
Your best resource for communicating with others is your own life and marriage. But as a couple, be sure that you agree about the issues and experiences you will share.

15. Do you have any additional tips for leading the group?

◆ Keep the focus on what the Scripture says, not on opinions.
◆ Seek for balanced group participation.
◆ Prioritize questions in advance.
◆ Be sensitive to couples who may be having marital problems.
◆ Consider co-leading with another couple.

APPENDIX C

LEADER'S NOTES

Session One

I Take You: Receiving Your Mate

Objectives

Session One sets the tone for *Keeping Your Covenant*, so try to make it fun and memorable. Do not allow the group to bog down in any area of discussion or linger on anything negative. Be sure that each person in the group has a copy of the study guide. Welcome the group members individually as they arrive and introduce those who do not know each other. Name tags may be helpful.

You will help your group members nurture oneness in their marriages as you guide them to:

- ◆ Affirm specific ways they and their mates need each other and can accept one another as God's gift.
- ◆ Analyze how weaknesses in their mates have an impact on how they receive them as God's provision.

Overall Comments

The **Warm Up** will encourage your group members to get to know each other a little better. Each couple will share their answers to the questions with the entire group. Whether or not they have met before, these questions should break the ice and help couples become more comfortable with each other.

Notes for the "Blueprints Section"

1. Couples often don't work as hard to please each other. Differences and small irritations become magnified after the excitement of courtship and early marriage begins to fade.

2. Matthew 7:24-27 speaks of our need to build our homes on a solid rock. This means focusing our lives on establishing a relationship with God and living our lives according to the principles He has put in the Bible. To be successful, a marriage must be built upon the rock of God and His Word.

3. Adam needed a mate, a companion, "a helper suitable for him" or "corresponding to him." "Alone" in this context is obviously a negative situation, since God specifically said it was "not good" and took action to remedy the problem.

4. To keep him from feeling self-sufficient. To enable him to recognize his need for God and for his mate, so that his mate would be able to provide for that which he lacked.

5. This helped Adam recognize that he did not have a suitable companion. There is no evidence Adam had any awareness of his need before then.

6. There is no right answer. Responses will vary for each individual or couple.

7. The five things referenced refer to:

◆ <u>Caused Adam to sleep</u>: Besides making the following surgical procedure easier, some people speculate that this step kept Adam from offering unwanted advice on the woman's design.

◆ <u>Took a rib</u>: This implies God recognized the equality of woman with man, as well as depicting the strong emotional bonds between the sexes.

◆ <u>Closed the flesh</u>: Adam was not harmed by this endeavor.

◆ <u>Made a woman</u>: She was totally God's handiwork.

◆ <u>Brought her to Adam</u>: God is obviously concerned about Adam's response to the woman and wanted her to be recognized as coming from Him.

8. He was completely aware of your needs. Your mate is God's provision for your needs.

9. Obviously, she was the only woman there, and we also can assume there was an immediate attraction between them. However, the only clue given in the passage is that Adam must have recognized that God was presenting her as a gift from Himself. He trusted in the God who had created him and who had now provided a mate for him.

10. There is no right answer. Responses will vary for each individual or couple.

11. No. Rejection of the gift is rejection of the Giver. The basis for my acceptance of my mate is faith in God's character and trustworthiness.

It's possible someone may ask, "When we were married, neither of us even knew God, let alone trusted Him. How could my mate be God's gift to me under that circumstance?" Refer the question to the group to answer. As you discuss this question, mention that the Scriptures clearly show that God is sovereign in the affairs of individuals and nations. Have the group look at Romans 8:28 to see the most common way God demonstrates His sovereignty: He shows His authority by turning even what is done in rebellion against Him into results that achieve His purposes. See Genesis 50:20.

If the issue of spouse abuse is raised, call attention to these Scriptures that provide wise counsel:

- Romans 13:1 and 1 Peter 2:13-15 teach God's establishment of governmental authority to control those who do wrong. A person in danger should not hesitate to contact the authorities for protection.

- Romans 5:8 shares Christ's example of loving the sinner even though hating sin (Psalm 45:7). One spouse's wrong acts do not excuse retaliation by the other.

- Proverbs 14:7 says to "leave the presence of a fool." This does not mean divorce; it simply advises establishing enough space to avoid the influence of the fool.

12. There is no right answer. Responses will vary for each individual or couple.

Session Two

To Be Your Husband/Wife: Comprehending Your Mate's Differentness

Objectives

You will help your group members increase their awareness and appreciation of male and female differences in marriage as you guide them to:

- Examine the biblical basis for male/female differences
- Discuss common misconceptions arising from male/female differences
- Study biblical instructions for how spouses are to respond to male/female differences in a marriage

Overall Comments

The main intent of this session is to build the understanding that many of the differences that exist in marriages are the result of male and female differentness. It was God who constructed men and women to be uniquely different from each other. Because these differences will not go away, the wise couple will acknowledge, understand, and even honor them.

To bring couples to a proper comprehension of some of these important male/female differences, an accurate understanding of statements in Scripture is necessary. It is crucial that group members recognize Scripture as the essential source of our understanding of human nature and its expression in male and female distinctives.

Be prepared to jump in and soften the atmosphere if the group becomes heated in its discussion. This may not happen, but a discussion about male/female differences often brings out some sharp disagreements.

Notes for the "Blueprints" Section

1. There is no right answer. Responses will vary for each individual or couple.

2. Understand your wife as a woman. Grant her honor as a fellow-heir of Jesus Christ.

3. It is "since she is a woman" that a man needs understanding into her thoughts and feelings. This recognition goes all the way back to God's original creation when He created both female and male as unique from the other.

4. There is no right answer. Responses will vary for each individual or couple.

5. If we live by our natural instincts doing what we think is right for us, we are in for trouble. Our natural instincts assume our mate thinks and feels the same way we do. We tend to treat our mate as we want to be treated, which in significant ways can be a great error. The way that seems right to us often does not honor our mate as a unique, special person, and the frequent end result of this path is conflict and abuse.

6. The feminist or women's liberation movement, which has voiced both valid and invalid grievances, can be viewed as a natural reaction to the failure of many husbands to honor their wives as equals and treat them as coheirs in life.

7. She is a fellow-heir of all that is good in life and should have an equal share of all that a couple experiences in their marriage.

8-9. There is no right answer. Responses will vary for each individual or couple.

Session Three

Love, Honor, and Cherish: Planting Positive Words

Objectives

You will help your group members strengthen their mates' self-esteem as you guide them to:

- Examine biblical and personal insights into the power of words

- Evaluate their expressions of praise to their mate
- Identify praiseworthy qualities possessed by their mate
- Practice expressing praise to their mate

Overall Comments

Collect the couples' lists of descriptive words or phrases. Randomly read these out loud and ask everyone to guess who is being described. This can be the most enjoyable session of the study, for its focus is highly positive. Everyone enjoys being complimented—even when they are embarrassed! Beyond making people feel good, positive words can have a lasting impact on an individual and on a marriage. In the opposite direction, negative words can have a profoundly harmful impact.

It is important to realize that some individuals and couples have long-established patterns of planting negative words—"weed seeds." The often-unintended harvest of such a pattern is the growth of negative, damaging attitudes. Being patient in seeing and responding to another person's life can literally help that person begin to turn around and start believing that real growth is possible.

Notes for the "Blueprints" Section

This **Blueprints** section focuses on the incredible power of words in influencing our mate's self-esteem. If you are aware of a couple in the group who tends to direct outbursts of anger at one another, you may need to ask the group for ideas of how to handle anger, bitterness, and a pattern of unkind ("cutting") remarks. You may want to invite comments on times when these outbursts tend to occur and suggestions on how to replace unkind words with comments that encourage.

1. The reality is that words can hurt you much more than sticks and stones. (It is not necessary to achieve agreement here. Simply get people to start thinking and talking.)

2. There is no right answer. Responses will vary for each individual or couple.

3. Proverbs 11:9—Words can destroy a person. Proverbs 12:25—The tongue has the power of death and life. Ephesians 4:29—A "good word" can lighten a heavy heart.

4. There is no right answer. Responses will vary for each individual or couple.

5. Because many married couples begin taking each other for granted, they fall into poor habits in how they relate to each other. Their hearts harden and they bury their hurts.

6. People can find it hard to give praise for several reasons: They have rarely received it, so they don't know how. They may feel they should praise others sparingly so that their position of authority and power is strengthened. Also, some find it easier to poke fun or disagree (especially in public) than to express affirmation and support. Sometimes this is a habit in which the person has good intentions, but simply does not feel comfortable directly expressing a positive emotion.

People can find it hard to receive praise if they sense the person's attitude is not one of honest appreciation. If a person's attitude and actions are not in tune, they sense they are being flattered or manipulated.

7-11. There is no right answer. Responses will vary for each individual or couple.

Session Four

To Have and to Hold: The Power of Prayer in Your Marriage

Objectives

You will help your group members discover the importance of prayer in spiritual growth as you guide them to:

- Recall what they learned about prayer as children
- Think of reasons why Christians don't pray more than they do
- Discover what the Bible says about the benefits of prayer
- Learn three components of prayer

- Understand how regularly praying together can change their marriage relationship

Notes for the "Blueprints" Section

1. Christians often have bad attitudes about prayer, and these attitudes keep them from praying more. They think prayer is boring, difficult, repetitive, ineffective. Some Christians wonder if prayer is really necessary; if God knows everything, why do we need to pray? Or they may wonder why God doesn't seem to answer their prayers more often. Another reason Christians may not pray is that they don't know how to do it.

2. Christian couples often know they should pray together, but they just don't do it. They don't make praying together a regular habit, and they let other activities and priorities take precedence. Another reason they may not pray is that they don't feel comfortable doing it.

3. Men often feel awkward, inadequate, and unsure of themselves. Men often like to be in charge, but prayer is not an activity in which they feel confident. Also, prayer may make them feel more vulnerable than they want to feel. And many men these days have grown up in homes where religion is considered "women's turf." Most wives love to pray with their husbands and may feel frustrated when their husbands don't take the lead in doing so.

4. John 16:24 invites us to ask our Father in heaven for whatever we need. It's like the blank check: "Ask, and you will receive." However, don't assume that God will grant any request we make of Him. We need to ask according to His will. Prayer also helps us grow in our relationship with God by giving us joy.

James 1:5 reminds us to look to God for wisdom. He will give us the type of wisdom that will greatly enrich our lives and help us with major and minor decisions.

5. It's a confidence builder. Specific answers to specific requests build our appreciation and level of confidence in God's great power and love in our lives.

6. There is no right answer. Responses will vary for each individual or couple.

7. Worship and praise raises our awareness of God's presence in our lives. The more we praise Him, the more we notice the ways He touches every aspect of our experience. Praising God also helps us see that our problems are more insignificant than we feel they are, that He will use even the worst problems to conform us to His image and that He is more powerful than our problems. Also, praising God for a specific quality you appreciate in your mate can be a powerful way to enrich a marriage. It is very hard to have an argument with someone for whom you have been praising God.

8. David felt defiled and guilty. He lost his joy in the Lord, and he felt dirty for what happened to him. He felt as if he were going to lose the very presence of God in his life.

David asked for forgiveness and cleansing, and we can assume that he received it from the Lord. He was given a renewed perspective on life, his responsibility to God, and the work of God in the world. Point out that most people review confession as a prelude to punishment. This is true in most areas of human experience. God's response is totally different.

9. He is faithful. He keeps His promises. He is just. Since Christ has already paid the penalty for our sins, God would be unjust not to forgive His children who have confessed their sins to Him.

10. This psalm not only talks about what God will do to answer our prayers, but it also discusses what He does in our hearts when we pray.

11. There is no right answer. Responses will vary for each individual or couple.

12. Matthew 7:7-11 indicates God's desire for us to make requests to Him. It also shows His desire to "give good gifts" to His children. Again, we shouldn't assume from this verse, that God will grant any request we make of Him. 1 John 5:14 shows that we need to ask "according to His will."

Since attending a FamilyLife Marriage Conference, the Martins' love really shows...

But who's keeping score?

FAMILYLIFE MARRIAGE CONFERENCE

Get away for a "Weekend to Remember"!

Chalk one up for your marriage! Get away to a FamilyLife Marriage Conference for a fun, meaningful weekend together. Learn how to understand your mate, build your marriage, and much more.

For more information or a free brochure, call 1-800-FL-TODAY.

We need your help!

Please take a few minutes to complete the evaluation form below and mail it to FamilyLife (P.O. Box 8220, Little Rock, AR 72221-8220). Your input is essential for us to determine the effectiveness of *Keeping Your Covenant*. We developed this introductory study to our HomeBuilders Couples Series® to encourage people to strengthen marriages through small groups. Thanks for making a difference!

Keeping Your Covenant Evaluation Form

Name: ______________________ E-mail: ______________________

Address: ____

City: ______________________ State: __________ ZIP: __________

Daytime Phone No.: (   )   - ______________ Evening Phone No.: (   )   - ______________

- How many HomeBuilders Couples Series have you led? ________
- Did you form this group using *Keeping Your Covenant*? Yes: _____ No: _____
  (If you answered yes, please answer the following questions.)
- How many people (total of individuals) are in your group? ________
- How would you rate this study?

	Poor									**Excellent**
Overall Experience	1	2	3	4	5	6	7	8	9	10
Study Guide Booklet	1	2	3	4	5	6	7	8	9	10

- Are you interested in leading another group/study? Yes: _____ No: _____
- Would you like information on HomeBuilders leadership training in your area? Yes: _____ No: _____

(To order HomeBuilders materials, or for more information, call FamilyLife at 1-800-FL-TODAY [1-800-358-6329], visit our Web site, www.familylife.com, or complete the order form on the back of this page.)

#HBKYC1

Choose ONE HomeBuilders Couples Series Study:
(Refer to pages 35-38 for descriptions of these resources.)

___ **Building Your Marriage***
___ **Building Teamwork in Your Marriage***
___ **Growing Together in Christ***
___ **Resolving Conflict in Your Marriage**
___ **Mastering Money in Your Marriage**
___ **Managing Pressure in Your Marriage**
___ **Building Your Mate's Self-Esteem***
___ **Life Choices for a Lasting Marriage**
___ **Expressing Love in Your Marriage**

Additional HomeBuilders Resources:

___ **Preparing for Marriage Couple's Pack**
___ **Preparing for Marriage Leader's Guide**
___ **Orientation Manual: An Introduction to HomeBuilders**
___ **Keeping Your Covenant** (a reproducible introductory study)

TO ORDER, CALL 1-800-FL-TODAY
Or complete this form and mail with payment to:
FamilyLife
P.O. Box 8220
Little Rock, AR 72221-8220

Choose the quantity and type:

Qty.	Price	Total	
____	$59.95	______	**HomeBuilders Starter Kit** Save 25% Leader's guide, seven study guides, video, orientation manual, and brochure
____	$19.95	______	**Leader's Pack** (one leader's guide and one study guide) Save $3.00
____	$16.95	______	**Couple's Pack** (two study guides) Save $3.00
____	$19.95	______	***Bible Study Electives** An all-in-one leader's guide with reproducible study handouts
____	$1.95	______	**HomeBuilders Orientation Manual**
____	$4.95	______	**Keeping Your Covenant**
____	$9.95	______	**Preparation for Marriage Leader's Guide**

________ Subtotal
________ Shipping
________ Tax-deductible donation
________ **GRAND TOTAL**

Shipping Charges:
Up to $20.00 . . . .$3.50
$20.01-$50.00 . . . .$5.50
$50.01-$75.00 . . . .$6.50
$75.01-$100.00 . . . . . .$7.50
over $100 . . . .$8.50

Name: ______________________
Address: ______________________
City: ____________ State: ____ ZIP: ________
Daytime Phone No.: ______________
____ My check is enclosed (payable to FamilyLife)
Charge to my ___ Visa ___ MasterCard ___ Discover
Card # ______ - ______ - ______ - ______ Exp. Date ____ / ____

Signature ______________________

#HBKYC1